325x

ABOUT THIS BOOK

IMMIGRATION looks at all aspects of an important and varied subject, which affects all of us in our everyday lives. This book will help you to understand the issues behind why people migrate and learn a little more about the consequences of immigration.

Throughout this book you will find information on many aspects of immigration – from its history to the laws governing it, from first hand accounts of migration to fascinating facts about individual countries.

© Aladdin Books Ltd 2004
Produced by
Aladdin Books Ltd
28 Percy Street
London W1T 2BZ

ISBN 0–7496–5519–4

First published in Great Britain in 2004 by
Franklin Watts
96 Leonard Street
London EC2A 4XD

Designers: Flick, Book Design and Graphics
Pete Bennett – PBD
Editor: Harriet Brown
Picture research: Brian Hunter Smart

The author, Ruth Wilson, is a researcher and writer on refugee and other issues. She has worked with the Refugee Coucil, the Refugee Arrivals Project and other refugee agencies.

Printed in Malaysia

06924

CONTENTS

3

INTRODUCTION

Immigration and asylum are often headline news. Wars and disasters result in mass movements of people. Companies get criticised for exploiting cheap immigrant workers. Asylum seekers are accused of being 'bogus'. Politicians win and lose votes because of their policies on immigration and refugees. International migration has changed the face of the world we live in and it is a trend that will continue.

This book takes a look at what is going on behind the statistics and the headlines, and sets out to answer some questions. Why do people move? Where do they come from and go to? How do they decide which country to go to? We will look at all forms of movement across borders, both long and short-term. We find out how people travel when they don't have the right documents, when they turn to smugglers or get tricked by people traffickers.

Many people, from all over the world, leave the country in which they were born to begin a new life in a new country.

There are likely to be many immigrants living and working in your neighbourhood.

Up to ten million people leave their country each year in search of a better life.

Children make up a large proportion of the global number of migrants.

WHAT DOES IMMIGRATION MEAN?

The word 'immigration' is used to describe the arrival of people who plan to settle in a country they weren't born in. International migration includes people who move to a new country and stay for the rest of their lives, or for a shorter time. Some travel to work abroad for a few months each year, and some cross a border every day to go to work. Events that have an impact on migration include war, ethnic conflict, repression, persecution and environmental disaster. Asylum seekers and refugees leave their country in order to survive.

People have always travelled
Across the centuries, humans have moved in search of opportunity, wealth, knowledge, security and freedom. They include: adventurers, seafarers, explorers, merchants, exiles, nomads, escaped criminals, prospectors, pioneers, slaves, missionaries, invaders, traders, mercenaries, colonisers and non-conformists.

5

More women and children are now crossing borders. We take a look at the dangers they face, especially when they are forced to flee because of war or persecution.

Some governments clamp down on immigration, and try to stop people from entering their borders. In this book, we explore the measures they adopt to manage migration. We also outline what people do once they arrive in another country and the kinds of work they take on. Finally, we look at what it means to go home. For some, this is returning to the country they first came from. For others, it means building a home in a new land, and possibly becoming a citizen there.

WHAT IS IMMIGRATION?

International migration takes place when you cross a border to settle in another country for a short time or for many years. An immigrant is an international migrant who has entered another country to live and work. Many words are used to describe people who cross borders, including settlers, contract workers, seasonal workers, professionals, illegal immigrants, economic migrants, asylum seekers and refugees.

What do the other names for immigrants mean?

Settlers – These are people who intend to live permanently in their new country.

Contract workers – These are workers who stay in a country while they do a particular piece of work.

Seasonal workers – Some industries need workers at a particular time of year, such as harvest time, when farms and food processing businesses need extra help.

Professionals – These include nurses, doctors, teachers, scientists, computer specialists, university lecturers and many others. Some are recruited by large organisations that have offices or factories in many countries.

Illegal immigrants – These are people who travel to work, but do not have the official papers needed to enter and stay in a country, such as a work permit, visa or passport. They get across borders without showing papers, or have false documents. They are often called undocumented workers.

Economic migrants – This term is used to describe anyone who travels legally to work. It does not include illegal immigrants, refugees and asylum seekers.

Asylum seekers – People who flee persecution and ask for asylum, or protection, in another country are called asylum seekers.

Refugees – Refugees are people who flee their homes in search of refuge, or safety, for example in times of war.

6

Illegal immigrants often have a long and dangerous journey to reach their destination country. Overcrowded boats can be very dangerous.

NUMBERS OF IMMIGRANTS

The number of international migrants has more than doubled in the last 35 years. In 1965, there were 75 million. In 2000, there were 175 million. In the same period, the world's population grew from 3 billion to 6 billion. Because the world's population growth is expected to slow down over the next few decades, the number of international migrants is likely to stay below 3 per cent, as you can see from the graph (right).

It is very hard to know exactly how many people move across borders each year.

Most people are on short-term trips, and are not counted as immigrants. International agencies believe that up to ten million people move between countries across the world each year.

World population
(in millions)

Non-migrants
Migrants

	8,770
	5,882
3,258	
1965	2000	2050
75 (2.3%)	175 (2.9%)	230 (2.6%)

Haiti is a country of emigration. People leave Haiti to enter the USA. Poverty, violence, instability and dictatorship have caused people to leave.

7

IMMIGRATION AND EMIGRATION

There are around 190 nation states in the world. They are all affected by international migration. Some are countries of 'emigration' – each year some of their citizens leave, to live in another country. Others are countries of 'immigration' – people arrive looking for a home and work within their borders.

Some countries are both. For example, migrants from some South American countries travel to Argentina to find work, but there is now an economic crisis in that country. This means that while newcomers arrive, Argentinians are leaving to find employment elsewhere.

Others are 'transit' countries – people travel through them on their way to their destination. African migrants, for example, travel by boat to the shores of Italy, and then head on to northern Europe.

WHERE DO PEOPLE COME FROM AND WHERE DO THEY GO?

Each year, around 2.3 million people move from the poorer, developing countries (such as countries in Africa, Latin America and Asia) to the developed countries (such as the USA, Canada, Australia and Europe).

Many more move from one developing country to another, and most move within one region. Colombians, for example, tend to go to Venezuela. Polish construction workers find work in Germany. At least half a million Burmese people are working in Thailand.

The top 5 countries of immigration (1970-1995)

United States of America	16.7 million
Russian Federation	4.1 million
Saudi Arabia	3.4 million
India	3.3 million
Canada	3.3 million

The top 5 countries of emigration (1970-1995)

Mexico	-6.0 million
Bangladesh	-4.1 million
Afghanistan	-4.1 million
Philippines	-2.9 million
Kazakhstan	-2.6 million

In 2003, the total number of refugees and displaced people worldwide was 20.6 million.

Map of some of the main migration movements

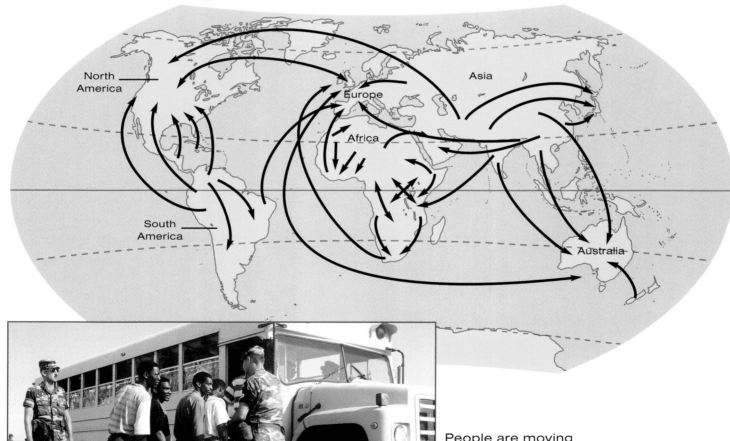

8

People are moving constantly in all directions all over the world.

One reason that people migrate is to escape poverty.

WHY DO PEOPLE MIGRATE?

Choosing to leave not just your home, but your country as well, is a big decision. You have to have strong reasons to want to leave your friends and family and the places you know to start a new life somewhere else.

The main reason that most people migrate is to get a better standard of living. Because of the differences in wealth between countries, migrants can improve their standard of living by moving.

Other reasons for migration are war, bad government, and environmental problems such as drought. Population increase is another pressure. The world population is growing by a net figure of 83 million people a year. Around 82 million are born in developing countries. So, more people are growing up in countries where there is not enough work to support them. Some travel abroad to make a living.

However, it is not the poorest people who choose to migrate. To travel any distance you have to have money. You need to be able to find out about the country you are going to. The poorest people don't have the education, contacts or money to do this.

THE GLOBAL ECONOMY

We now live in a global economy. Countries and continents trade with each other. Companies open factories where labour is cheap.

In the 1970s, oil-producing countries became very wealthy. There were more jobs than workers, and countries such as Saudi Arabia and Iran attracted millions of workers from other Arab states, from the Indian subcontinent and from Asia.

In the 1980s, the economies of Singapore, Taiwan, South Korea and Hong Kong improved. Koreans, who had been travelling to the oil-producing countries to work, found there were more jobs at home.

Since the 1990s, and the break-up of the Soviet empire, there are now more countries in the world, and more international borders. China has become part of the global economy. Many more people are leaving China – and many more people are going there from other countries. International migration is now part of our world and is here to stay.

9

A short history

People have always moved. Before the 19th century, many countries did not have clearly defined frontiers, and it was easy to cross from one into another. But most people did not move away from the town or village they were born in. In Europe in the 19th century, there were mass movements of people. New industries and cities were developing, and people found they could no longer live off the land. People moved to the cities, but there was not enough work. People left Europe to live in North America.

From the start of the 20th century, the number of people migrating has steadily increased. Countries that had been colonies became independent. People moved to look for work. Newspapers, radio and TV meant that people in poorer countries learnt more about life in other countries.

Is immigration a good thing or a bad thing?

There is a lot of debate surrounding migration. Is it good or bad? Different people and countries have different views. These are some of the things people say, both for and against immigration.

Against immigration

There is not enough work to go round, so the people who arrive are often unemployed.

Immigrants take the jobs of local people. They make some of the citizens of their new country unemployed.

Because they work for low pay, immigrants push wages down. This means local people also end up working for less money.

They don't contribute to the economy. They avoid paying taxes.

Immigrants live off the government. They use schools and hospitals and are a drain on resources.

Some countries are overcrowded. There isn't room for more people.

Immigration can lead to racism and violence. Immigrants cause disruption by getting into crime.

In the country they come from, immigrants are often the more wealthy and enterprising people – they are needed at home to help their nation prosper.

For immigration

Immigrants often do the dirty, dangerous and low-paid jobs that local people do not want to do. They also fill the shortage of skilled workers, such as doctors and nurses.

Immigrants create work – they eat at cafes, catch buses and trains, and spend their money at shops. Many set up their own businesses.

Because many work for low wages, immigrants help keep down the cost of living. They enable local people to get better jobs. For example, low-paid immigrant nannies and au pairs enable mothers to take on higher-paid work.

Over time, immigrants and their descendants make a major contribution to the economy of their new country.

Only some immigrants are supported by the government through welfare benefits. Most earn money through working. Often, they help run hospitals and schools.

Developed countries often have ageing populations and a decreasing birth rate. They need people to come in to keep the economy going.

Having a mix of people enriches the life of a nation. Immigrants bring their music, art and their ways of cooking to their new country. Most immigrants want to live peacefully and within the law.

Many immigrants send money home, making a significant contribution to the economy of their country of origin.

CHOOSING TO MOVE

Most international migrants choose whether they will leave their home and where they will go. This is called voluntary migration. Some people have no choice. They flee their country because of war, famine or persecution. This is called forced migration. Most people who are forced to migrate are refugees.

Environmental problems, such as drought, can cause people to flee their home.

CHOOSING TO MIGRATE

If you were thinking about moving to a new country, there would be many things to consider.

Where could you get work?

You must find out where there is a demand for the job you do. Doctors, nurses and teachers are needed in many different countries. However, qualifications gained in one country are not always recognised in another. You may not be able to carry on in the same line of work. You may need to look at what jobs you are willing to do. Sometimes highly-skilled people do low-paid work in order to settle somewhere else.

How much better off would you be?

Once you've identified a few possible countries, you'll need to find out what earnings and the cost of living are like. A salary may look much higher, but basic living costs may be higher as well, so will you be better off? You may also want to send some money home to your relatives as well as have a better lifestyle.

Some people are forced to move to a new country.

How to get to the new country is another important consideration for most migrants.

It can be very hard to get official documents.

What language?

People often go to a country where they speak the same language. Many people know some English, and therefore pick an English-speaking country. Some languages are easier to learn than others.

Do you have enough money?

You want to be sure you can afford the journey, and have enough to tide you over on arrival. If you're lucky, your ticket will be paid for by an employer, but many people save up for years to pay for their journey. Some get into debt with people-smugglers, and end up working for gangs doing low-paid jobs, or for no pay at all.

Do you have the right documents?

Some countries want immigrants with certain skills, and will arrange for them to get work permits and visas. It can be very hard to get official documents. Many people travel with false papers, or enter another country secretly, with no documents at all.

Do you know anyone already in the country?

Many people travel to a country where a friend or a relative is living. They will have a roof over their heads when they arrive. Their friend will introduce them to other people, and may help them get a job.

A migrant's story

Artan is 23 years old, and from Albania. He graduated from secondary school, but there is little work in his country and he couldn't find a job. He decided to migrate, and crossed illegally into Macedonia, which is near his hometown.

In Macedonia, he looked for work for a couple of weeks but found nothing. By this time, he had spent all his money. He decided to go to Greece, because he'd heard that the pay was better there and that there were more opportunities. He ended up working on a farm.

He worked for a few months and saved up some money. But one day the police stopped him and found that he had no documents. He was taken to the police station and beaten. The next day they escorted him back to Albania. Artan was lucky. When he got home, he got a place on an official migration programme and went to work in Italy.

12

Are there any migrant networks?

There may be people in the new country from the same place as you. They will speak the same language, give advice on how to travel and help you to find your feet when you arrive.

Is there somewhere nearby to go?

It's cheaper and easier to travel a short distance. People travel on a daily basis into Switzerland and Luxembourg to work, crossing the border again each evening to go home. With many cheap flights now on offer in Europe, some people spend Monday to Friday in one country, and go home for the weekend in another.

The internet-based email service – Hotmail – was invented by an immigrant.

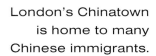

London's Chinatown is home to many Chinese immigrants.

MAKING A BIG SUCCESS

A few immigrants are extraordinarily successful. Sabeer Bhatia grew up in the Indian city of Bangalore. He did really well at school, and at the age of 19 he went to study in the USA. When he arrived, he had just 250 dollars in his pocket. After studying computers and technology, he went to work with a computer company. Then he came up with an idea for a simple, free and secure way of talking on the internet. He called it Hotmail. Two years later, he sold it to Microsoft for a reported 400 million dollars.

A family of migrants

Winston left the Caribbean island of Barbados when he was 14, to join his mother. She had moved to the UK ten years earlier, when the British government was recruiting workers from the Caribbean.

Winston was able to enter the country legally because he was joining his mother. He went to school and university in the UK. Then he moved to Guyana to teach for a few years. He met and married a Guyanese woman, Andrea, and they returned to the UK together. Their long-term plan is to go and live in Barbados.

13

FORCED TO MIGRATE

Refugees are people who have fled their country and who cannot return because they will be in danger if they do. They may be in danger because of their political views. They could be persecuted because of their race, religion or nationality, or because they belong to a particular social group.

Conditions can often be harsh for people forced from their homes.

Asylum seekers are people who have fled their country of origin and have asked for asylum. Worldwide, more than one million people requested asylum in 2002, or were waiting for a decision. The single biggest number was 59,000 Iraqis, escaping repression and war in their country.

In the last 50 years, several million people have been granted asylum.

Refugee rights

In 1948, the United Nations (UN) agreed the Universal Declaration of Human Rights. Article 14 of the Declaration says that everyone has the right "to seek and to enjoy in other countries asylum from persecution". This means that victims of human rights abuses must be able to leave their country freely and seek refuge elsewhere.

In 1951, the Office of the United Nations High Commissioner for Refugees (UNHCR) was created to help refugees. In the same year, the UN adopted the 'Convention Relating to the Status of Refugees'. This convention defines the rights of refugees. It also outlines the responsibilities of governments to offer protection to refugees. It is often called the Geneva Convention, after the place where it was signed.

Government delegates and representatives of international organisations discuss migration and refugee issues in Geneva, Switzerland.

WHERE DO REFUGEES COME FROM?

Refugees come from all over the world. Many are from countries where there are repressive governments or war. Not everyone in need of asylum escapes. Some governments imprison and even kill people who oppose them.

Palestinians are the largest group of refugees in the world today. When Israel was founded in 1948, 80 per cent of Palestinians left. There are around 3.8 million Palestinian refugees. Most of them are in Jordan, Gaza and the West Bank. Others are in neighbouring countries.

Over more than 20 years of war, more than four million Afghans have fled their country. Many are still in exile, most are in Iran and Pakistan.

HOT SPOTS

Many countries are unstable and dangerous. From some, only limited numbers of people escape. But sometimes, many people flee in a short period of time.

Many thousands of Afghan refugees are in Pakistan.

Democratic Republic of the Congo

Thousands have fled the Democratic Republic of the Congo. Since 1997, war has devastated the country. There are numerous groups fighting, and terrible atrocities have been carried out. Thousands of civilians have been killed or injured. The surrounding countries are also war torn and refugees have also entered the Democratic Republic of the Congo.

Liberia

More than 100,000 Liberians have fled their country in recent years. President Charles Taylor was in power from 1997-2003. He attacked and imprisoned anyone who criticised his government. Fighters for and against the government looted, raped and killed people. Charles Taylor is now in exile in Nigeria, but the situation in Liberia remains unstable.

Iraq

In 2002, Iraq was the top refugee-producing country in the world. At least 400,000 Iraqis live as refugees or asylum seekers in 90 countries. More than 200,000 are in Iran, and many others are in Europe and the USA. They fled war and the brutal regime of Saddam Hussein, who was captured by the Americans in December 2003.

Where are most of the world's refugees? (2002)	
Iran	1.3 million
Pakistan	1.2 million
Germany	980,000
Tanzania	690,000
USA	485,000
Serbia and Montenegro	350,000
Democratic Republic of the Congo	330,000
China	300,000
Armenia	250,000

15

ASYLUM CLAIMS IN THE DEVELOPED COUNTRIES

Most of the world's refugees go to developing countries, but many request asylum in developed nations. In 2002, the five developed countries that received the highest number of claims were the UK (110,700), USA (81,100), Germany (71,000), France (50,800) and Canada (33,400).

Another way to look at the figures is to compare the number of asylum seekers with the size of the country's population. Austria is then at the top of the list. This is because in 2002, it had 4.6 asylum applicants for every 1,000 inhabitants.

Many people request asylum in developed nations.

Refugee stories

Tiawan Gongloe is a leading Liberian human rights lawyer. He often spoke out against abuses carried out by the government and the rebel forces. He was arrested for speaking publicly about the violence. A newspaper that printed his speech was shut down. He was beaten so badly that he was unable to stand. He was taken to hospital. He was afraid he would be arrested and tortured again when he left hospital. A human rights group helped him and his family leave Liberia. He is now a refugee in the USA.

Golnaz left Iran when she was 20. Her father had been put in prison for his political activities. A friend she went to school with was shot for selling a political newspaper. Her neighbours were executed. Golnaz was frequently stopped on the streets and harassed. Young women were not allowed out with young men – when she went shopping with her brother, they were both detained and interrogated. Golnaz had money and a passport, and the family agreed that she should escape. She went to Sweden, where she gained asylum.

HOW GOVERNMENTS REACT

Most governments ask people to prove that their fear of persecution is justified. Some governments take in many refugees. Others have little choice – if their country shares a border with a war zone, it is hard to stop people crossing.

But in recent years, many governments have made it much more difficult for people to enter their country and ask for asylum. They see refugees as a threat or a burden. Since the September 2001 terrorist attacks on the US, a number of countries have pushed through emergency anti-terrorism legislation which limits the rights of asylum seekers. Human rights groups say that many governments are not respecting their obligation to give protection to refugees.

MISUSE OF THE SYSTEM

Some countries restrict the number of legal migrants who can enter and work. People who are not escaping persecution ask for asylum as a way to get in and find a job. Their misuse of the asylum system can make it harder for genuine refugees to find safety.

FAMOUS REFUGEES OF OUR TIME

Many famous people have been refugees. They include the physicist Albert Einstein (left), the psychoanalyst Sigmund Freud, the philosopher Hannah Arendt, the author Isabel Allende and the filmstar Andy Garcia.

Miriam Makeba

In the 1950s, singer Miriam Makeba appeared in a powerful anti-apartheid TV documentary in her home country, South Africa. As a result, she was invited to visit Europe and America. But because of the documentary, the South African government took away her citizenship. She was not allowed back.

In 1963, she testified about apartheid before the UN. But in 1968, after marrying a radical black activist, her American concerts were cancelled and her recording contract was broken. She went to live in the African country of Guinea. When the apartheid regime ended in the 1990s, Miriam Makeba was able to go home.

The Dalai Lama

His Holiness the Dalai Lama Tenzin Gyatso is the head of state and spiritual leader of the Tibetan people. He became leader at the age of 15, when the Chinese invaded Tibet. The Tibetans were opposed to Chinese rule, and a resistance movement spread across the country. The uprising was crushed by the Chinese army and the Dalai Lama escaped to India where he was given political asylum. Some 80,000 Tibetan refugees followed him into exile.

Edward Said

Edward Said was born in Jerusalem, to a Christian family. When Israel was founded in 1948 they were forced to leave, and went to live in Egypt. Later he moved to the USA, where he became a university professor.

For many years he was the leading US advocate for the Palestinian cause. His books have been translated into 26 languages. He was a prominent member of the Palestinian parliament-in-exile for 14 years. His outspoken position made him many enemies. He suffered repeated death threats. In 1985 he was called a Nazi by the Jewish Defence League and his university office was set on fire.

He also wrote about art and helped found an orchestra which brought young Palestinian and Israeli musicians together. He died in 2003.

The Dalai Lama fled Tibet in 1959. In 1989 he was given the Nobel Peace Prize for his work on human rights.

MAKING THE JOURNEY

For some migrants, the journey to a new country can be long and difficult.

For some people, the journey to another country is short and straightforward. Aeroplanes have made international travel for legal migrants relatively easy. However, asylum seekers fleeing persecution, and people who have not got the right documents, face much more hazardous journeys.

As the numbers of people moving round the world has increased, migration has become big business. There are people and companies who offer help to would-be immigrants by arranging their travel and sometimes by finding work for them as well. Some are legal, some are not. Travelling with the illegal operators – the traffickers and people smugglers – can be very dangerous.

Aeroplanes have made international travel much easier for some migrants.

SMUGGLING

Smugglers make a lot of money from getting people into countries without going through border controls. They hide people in lorries, give them false documents, or bribe immigration officers. Smuggling is profitable because, while many developed countries need more workers, there are few opportunities to get there legally. So people wanting such work find illegal ways to get in. It is big business: in Russia alone there are around 450,000 illegal migrants, many of whom are trying to travel westward.

Chinese gangs, called 'snakeheads', are known to run routes over several borders. This can be very dangerous. In 2000, 58 Chinese migrants were discovered dead in a lorry at Dover in the UK. They had suffocated while trapped in a container. Other gangs arrange sea crossings from North Africa to Spain. Smugglers often insist that the passengers swim the last stretch. At least 200 people are thought to drown each year on this route.

TRAFFICKING

Smugglers help people who want to migrate. Trafficking takes place through trickery or force. Traffickers threaten people, abduct them or trick them into travelling.

Between one and two million people are trafficked each year, and most are women and children. They end up working in the sex industry, or as slaves in domestic service and other forms of work. They are abused, humiliated and exploited. It can be very difficult to trap these criminals, because the victims are so hidden and so powerless.

Thousands of migrants are smuggled across borders each year. The conditions can be very dangerous.

FROM MEXICO INTO THE USA

The border between the USA and Mexico is one of the most frequently crossed borders in the world. People walk across the desert, crawl through drainage pipes and float across the Rio Grande on tyre inner tubes. Between 1998 and 2001, more than 1,500 people died trying to enter the USA – most of them from heatstroke and dehydration.

The smugglers on this crossing are called 'coyotes'. Their fee varies, depending on whether they leave the person just inside the USA, or help them to travel further north. The border is heavily policed on the American side, with high fences and helicopter controls. However, the border is so long that it is always possible to find a more remote place to cross over.

Since the terrorist attacks on the USA on September 11, 2001, the American authorities have introduced more penalties for people caught entering illegally.

19

Smuggled to safety

Mohammed fled Afghanistan when his brother was forced to fight for the Taliban. He got a car to the border with Iran where about 150 other young men had gathered to escape. They walked for three days through the mountains towards Turkey. At the Turkish border, guards caught many of the group. Mohammed crossed by foot into Bulgaria and hid on a train going to Greece. He paid smugglers for the final stages of the journey. A plane took him to Sarajevo. He then spent hours hidden in the back of a lorry. He finally reached the UK and asked for asylum.

Victim of trafficking

Louisa grew up in the Dominican Republic. When she was 17, a woman from Argentina offered her work as a domestic servant. Louisa was young and poor, and she accepted. When she arrived in Argentina, she was taken to an apartment where there were many other girls. Louisa realised they were working as prostitutes. She tried to leave, but was told she owed money for the airfare. She didn't even have enough to phone home. She was forced to work as a prostitute. Louisa was saved when an outsider stepped in to help. An international agency got her home, where a health project helped her recover.

WAR AND IMMIGRATION

Many people flee war-torn countries. Some wars go on for many years, and large numbers leave. Wars today are different to those of 50 years ago. In the First and Second World Wars, most of the casualties were soldiers. Today, most of the people injured and killed are civilians. People try to escape the violence and the human rights abuses. They also leave because war brings poverty and hunger. At times of war, crops are destroyed and businesses are forced to close.

Most of the wars today are civil wars – they take place within one country rather than between countries. Wars are mainly concentrated in the world's poorest nations, where there is little democracy or dictators are in power. As long as there is poverty, injustice and competition for limited resources, it is likely that wars will break out and there will be refugees.

Countries involved in war and civil war, 1997-2004

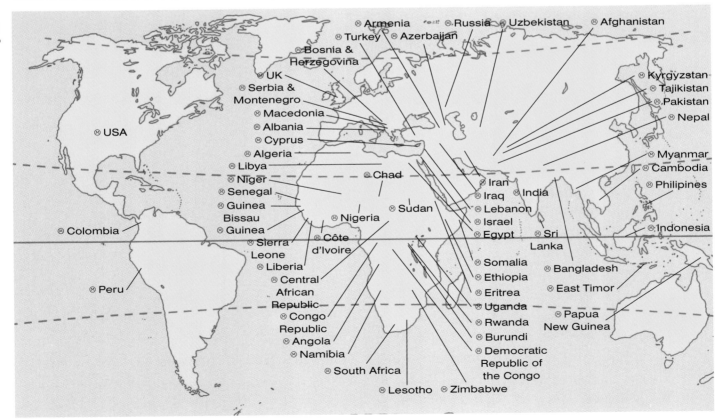

ESCAPING WAR

Civilians who flee fighting are very vulnerable. Often, they have to abandon their homes with no warning, losing all their possessions. They have little choice in how they travel and where they travel to. Most do not go far – they try to get across the nearest border to safety.

Often the journey itself is dangerous. For example, around 65,000 Sudanese refugees fled to eastern Chad in 2002. They had been walking for many days. They were in poor health: they escaped during the rainy season, and many suffered from exposure, pneumonia and other illnesses. During the journey they were targeted by gunfire from aircraft.

Some war refugees travel further. In 2001, Afghans applied for asylum in at least 76 countries across the world including Brazil, Cuba and Singapore. Many arrived in Europe seeking safety.

War can devastate towns and cities, causing people to flee their country.

Refugee camps aren't always safe places to stay. Women and children are particularly at risk of abuse.

REFUGEE CAMPS

Millions of refugees who escape war end up in refugee camps in nearby countries. Some are makeshift and not officially recognised. Usually, governments and aid agencies work with the UNHCR to set up and run the camps. Food, water and shelter are arranged. In long-term camps, projects are set up to help people become more self-supporting.

While some camps are well organised, others are centres of poverty. The inhabitants are often women and children who arrive with nothing but the clothes they're wearing. They are housed in tents. Some people spend decades living in camps – there are Afghans who arrived in camps in Pakistan as children and have grown up there.

Camps may be targeted by armed forces. In some, there is little law and order. Sometimes, the host country gives only limited support, and may try to shut the camp down.

For the refugees, there are three ways out. They may be able to go home one day, they may be allowed to leave the camp and live freely in the country they have reached, or they may be helped to move on to safety in another country.

21

Conditions in many refugee camps are terrible. They are usually very overcrowded. Camps are hard to police so there is little law and order.

Thousands of Burundians have fled to Tanzania.

LIFE IN A REFUGEE CAMP

As a result of its conflict with Armenia, Azerbaijan has 750,000 refugees living within its borders. The two countries are fighting for control of the refugees' small homeland, Nagorno Karabakh.

Conditions in the camps are terrible. Most are towns of makeshift huts and tent-like dwellings, with no surfaced roads. In winter, the camp becomes a sea of mud. The huts are made out of materials the refugees have scavenged, such as corrugated iron.

The buildings are usually overcrowded and have no running water or sewage systems. Electricity supplies are erratic. Children receive little education. Health care is basic. Diarrhoea is widespread, and many people are ill because they are undernourished.

One camp is in a railway station, where 400 people live in rusting old goods wagons, which become baking hot in the sun. They hope that one day a train will be hitched up to the wagons and take them home. Some people have been in the camps for seven years.

TANZANIA: HOME TO THOUSANDS FLEEING WAR

Tanzania is the neighbour of a number of warring countries. For more than seven years, it has been a safe haven for hundreds of thousands of refugees.

• 300,000 Burundians have fled the civil war in their country, escaping into Tanzania.

• There are 120,000 refugees in Tanzania from the conflict in the Democratic Republic of the Congo.

• In the 1990s, half a million Rwandans escaped to Tanzania. Some have now returned.

Huge camps have been set up to house many of the refugees. But Tanzania has its own problems: droughts and floods have caused widespread food shortages. The refugees are resented by local people who themselves don't have enough to eat.

CHILD SOLDIERS

There are some 300,000 child soldiers around the world. They have been forced to join armies and rebel groups, where they suffer terrible abuses. Some children flee their country to avoid this happening to them, while others manage to escape after being forced to fight. They need special care but it is hard for them to find a safe haven.

Children have been forced to work as soldiers in Sierra Leone. Some of them have escaped and found a safe haven where they can rebuild their lives.

The rights of people fleeing war

Some governments question whether civilians fleeing war should be considered refugees. The 1951 Geneva Convention, which defines refugee law, does not include them. However, the UNHCR says that if their country is unwilling or unable to protect them, people escaping war should be considered refugees.

To keep their refugee status, they must remain civilians. People who flee and then take up arms against their country of origin are considered soldiers and not refugees.

AVOIDING CONSCRIPTION

Every country has the right to ask its citizens to join the armed forces at times of war. This is called conscription. However, citizens also have the right to refuse if they believe war is wrong – if they are pacifists, for example. Such people are called conscientious objectors. In some countries, conscientious objectors have been treated very badly, and some have been killed. People who are persecuted because they are conscientious objectors have the right to claim asylum in another country.

WAR CRIMINALS

Terrible crimes are committed in wars. The UN has agreed rules stating what can and cannot be done in war. These are often broken.

People who carry out war crimes are criminals. If their side is losing, some escape – often by pretending to be ordinary refugees. After the Rwandan war, people who had committed terrible atrocities were living in the huge refugee camps in neighbouring countries. Efforts are made to find such people and bring them to justice. War criminals are not entitled to be refugees.

Refugee camps run by aid organisations and the UNHCR are there to look after genuine refugees, not war criminals.

RACE, ETHNICITY & IMMIGRATION

Today, most countries have mixed populations which include people from different races and ethnic groups. In many, more than a third of the population is made up of minority ethnic groups.

Most schools in the UK contain pupils from many different ethnic backgrounds.

Proportion of people from ethnic, racial or national minorities in the population

More than 50%	Afghanistan, India, Indonesia, Iran, Kazakhstan, Peru, and many African nations
30%-50%	Bangladesh, Belgium, Brazil, Colombia, Jamaica, Mexico, Morocco, Malawi, Malaysia, Mozambique, Pakistan, Thailand, Ukraine, Venezuela
10%-29%	Canada, Russia, Saudi Arabia, South Africa, Spain, Sweden, the US, Vietnam, Zimbabwe
Below 10%	Argentina, Australia, China, Egypt, Japan, the UK, and many other European countries

STIRRING UP HATRED

It is more common for ethnic groups to live together peacefully than in a state of conflict. But political leaders can stir up hatred between groups in order to gain more power. They encourage people to feel threatened by anyone who is different.

In some countries, minority groups have their human rights removed. They may be barred from travelling or owning property, or entering into certain kinds of employment or education.

Racism and ethnic conflict can also lead to mass persecution, atrocities, civil war and even genocide. Genocide is the killing of everyone who belongs to a particular group. Countries where people are being persecuted because of their race or ethnicity include Uganda, Burma, Indonesia and Russia. In these conditions, many people flee to find safety in other countries.

LOOKING FOR SAFETY

People fleeing ethnic and racial violence do not always find safety in the countries that they move to. Roma people fleeing Kosovo, for example, face hostility and prejudice in many countries.

Migrants who are not fleeing ethnic persecution can still find themselves in danger in their new country because of their race or ethnic group. The Côte d'Ivoire is a country of immigrants. About one quarter of its people are from abroad or are descended from immigrants, yet since 2002 they have suffered violent attacks and abuse. In some European countries, extreme right wing and racist groups have gained popularity because of fears of immigration.

In the long run, immigration is adding to the diversity of all countries. Because of migration, we will meet more people from different backgrounds, and the traditional boundaries between languages, cultures and ethnic groups will gradually change.

Some examples of where racism has led to immigration.

Bhutan: Ethnic expulsion

In the early 1990s, the Bhutanese government forced more than 100,000 people to leave. Most were ethnic Nepalese. They were told they were no longer Bhutanese citizens, and had their nationality taken away from them. This is one of the largest ethnic expulsions in modern history. The refugees have been living in camps in south-eastern Nepal ever since.

Rwanda: Planned genocide

In the mid-1990s, extremists in the Hutu government brutally slaughtered Tutsis and Hutus who opposed their regime. In a six-week period in 1994, specially trained army units and the militia massacred 800,000 people. Over two years, nearly two million Rwandans fled to neighbouring countries.

Iraq: Mass persecution

For 23 years, Saddam Hussein used his security services and army to imprison, torture and persecute Kurds in northern Iraq. He also persecuted the Shi'a community and other minority groups. In 1988, the Iraqi forces dropped mustard gas and nerve gas on the Kurdish town of Halabja, killing at least 5,000 people. In 2003, more than 500,000 Iraqis were living in exile.

Bosnia-Herzegovina: Ethnic cleansing

Serbian forces used massacre, terror and rape for 'ethnic cleansing' of large areas of the multi-ethnic republic of Bosnia-Herzegovina. Later, Bosniak and Bosnian-Croatian forces also committed atrocities. In the worst single incident, Bosnian-Serb forces killed over 7,000 Bosniak men in the small town of Srebrenica in June 1995. Many refugees fled to other countries (below).

25

POLITICS & IMMIGRATION

Most people migrate for economic reasons – to have a better standard of living. Economic stability and prosperity are more likely to be found in stable democracies, and so some people head for countries where there are elected governments. But this is not the only reason and people also move to countries where the political situation is not so secure.

Many asylum seekers, however, are fleeing because of politics. They are forced to leave countries that are run by dictators, or where the political system is corrupt or weak. Some are political leaders themselves – but not all. They may simply belong to an opposition party that is suddenly outlawed, or they may take part in a peaceful protest and face arrest. In some countries, elections take place but are rigged – people can be attacked and even imprisoned for voting in the 'wrong' way, or for failing to vote.

Sometimes, family members are persecuted because they are related to a political activist. Women often have to flee if their husbands are imprisoned, killed or forced into hiding.

Over the last decade, thousands of Zimbabweans have fled the oppressive regime of the president, Robert Mugabe.

ZIMBABWE

President Robert Mugabe, who has ruled Zimbabwe for more than 20 years, is a strong and ruthless leader, deeply intolerant of dissent – refusal to conform to authority – and opposition.

In 2002, his government ordered a huge crackdown on people who supported other parties. Government-led violence spread from rural areas into towns and cities. Hundreds claimed they had been beaten and tortured. The authorities also discriminated against anyone they considered a political opponent by denying them access to food programmes. Political activists are among the many people who have asked for asylum outside the country.

CHINA

In recent years, China has become one of the world's leading economic powers, but political opponents of China's government are imprisoned without a fair trial. Hundreds of people are executed every year. The authorities have blocked internet search engines, closed publications, harassed journalists, tightened controls on satellite transmission, and hampered the work of academics and activists.

In 2002, one person was sentenced to 11 years in prison for downloading 'counter-revolutionary' leaflets from the web and publishing them in book form. More people are now escaping China – in the year 2000, around 18,000 Chinese people requested asylum in Europe.

EAST TIMOR

José Ramos-Horta is a political leader who endured years of exile because of his beliefs. Born in East Timor, as a young man he worked as a journalist and got involved in politics.

East Timor was a colony of Portugal, and he became one of the leaders of the campaign for independence. When the Portuguese left in 1974, he was made a Minister in the new government. The next year, while he was travelling abroad, Indonesia invaded East Timor. He could not go back.

He spent the next 23 years in exile, speaking out against the Indonesian occupation. He went to the UN, and helped get a peace plan started. In 1996, he was awarded the Nobel Peace Prize.

In May 2002, East Timor became an independent country, with Ramos-Horta as Foreign Minister. He was finally able to go home.

Foreign-born politicians

Many immigrants remain interested in the politics of their country of origin, and some actively campaign for political change. Some become politicians in their new country.

The movie star Arnold Schwarzenegger is one example. He was born in a small, isolated village in Austria. He took up body building as a way of getting a better life. He became the world champion, but his goal was to move to America and be a film actor. He went there in 1970, when he was 23, and got a role starring in a movie. He went on to become a top Hollywood star. In 1984 he became a US citizen. In 2003 he was elected governor of California.

Madeleine Albright, the former Secretary of State for the USA, is an immigrant.

Another example is Madeleine Albright, who was sworn in as the first woman Secretary of State in the USA in 1997. This is one of the most senior posts in the US government. She was born in Czechoslovakia, in 1937. Her family fled to England to escape the Nazi rise to power. When she was 11 she reached the USA, where her father requested asylum for the family. As an adult, she became a US citizen. Neither Madeleine Albright nor Arnold Schwarzenegger can become President of the United States. At the moment, you have to be a US-born citizen to do that.

RELIGION & IMMIGRATION

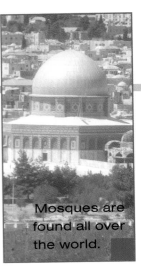

Mosques are found all over the world.

Over the centuries, religions have spread across the world through the movement of people. The Jewish people, through hundreds of years of trade, travel and persecution, have spread across the globe. During the Second World War, the Nazi regime in Germany massacred about six million Jews. Many thousands fled to other countries. The state of Israel was founded, and now encourages immigration by Jews.

Religion remains an important force in attitudes to immigration. After September 11, for instance, there has been a growth in hostility towards Muslims. Known as 'Islamophobia', it has led to violent attacks on immigrants in some countries.

Sikhism is a religion practised in many parts of the world. Sikhism originally comes from India.

Hindus form the largest religious group in India. Hinduism has spread across the world.

Denying the right to believe

Article 18 of the UN Declaration of Human Rights states that everyone has the right to freedom of thought, conscience and religion. They also have the right to worship on their own or with other people, and to change their religion or beliefs.

Over the years, many people have been forced to leave their country because of their religious beliefs.

• In 2003, thousands of Hindus fled from Bangladesh to India, claiming that they were being persecuted on religious and political grounds.

• Many thousands of Bosnian Muslims were slaughtered or forced from their home during the Serbian invasion of their land. Others went into exile.

• In Iran, Jews, Baha'is and Sufis have been persecuted. Some have left the country.

• During the US bombing of Afghanistan in 1991, members of the small Sikh community fled to Pakistan, taking their holy books with them for safekeeping.

FINDING A SAFE HAVEN

Around 1,000 members of a remote Vietnamese hill tribe fled to Cambodia in 2001 claiming that the government was carrying out a crackdown on ethnic and religious minorities. The hill people, known as Montagnards, are mostly Christian. The Vietnamese government was taking away their farmland, and abusing them. Christmas church services were banned to prevent large gatherings.

REBUILDING A COMMUNITY

In 1989, there were just 6,000 Jews in Berlin. The number has now doubled – Germany has the world's fastest-growing Jewish community. Most come from the former Soviet Union. They don't have to apply for asylum: all they need is an identity card from the former Soviet Union marked with the letter 'J'. The old Jewish quarter of Berlin is thriving again.

However, there have been anti-Semitic attacks, so the police guard synagogues and Jewish businesses.

FACING A FORCED RETURN

The Burmese military government has been condemned for its treatment of minority religious groups. In the 1990s, about 250,000 Muslim Rohingya refugees crossed into Bangladesh to escape persecution. They said their land had been confiscated and they were being pressed into forced labour.

They were placed in large camps. Many returned to Burma when the UN stepped in to help, but some went back to Bangladesh saying there had been no improvement. By 2003, there were 20,000 refugees enduring very difficult camp conditions. The Bangladeshi government was aiming to return them all and shut down the camps.

After the Second World War many Jews left their homes to emigrate to Israel.

In some countries, police are needed to protect religious minorities.

WOMEN & IMMIGRATION

Today, many women migrate to other countries. In the past, when women moved from one country to another, they usually travelled with their family. The man aimed to be the main breadwinner. Now, more women are travelling on their own, and more women are travelling in order to earn money for their families.

Nearly half of all international migrants are women. In some regions the figure is higher. In Asia, most of the migrants working overseas are women. In 1999, around 65 per cent of all overseas workers from Sri Lanka were female. In the Philippines, some 70 per cent of migrants going abroad to work were women.

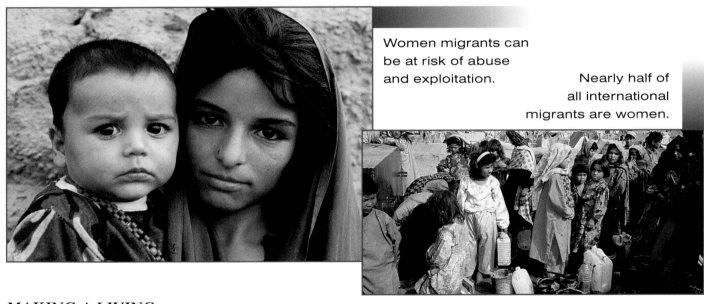

Women migrants can be at risk of abuse and exploitation.

Nearly half of all international migrants are women.

MAKING A LIVING

Migration can be a positive experience for women. If they get work, it can give them independence. They may get training or qualifications, and increase their skills and earning potential. But it is not always good news. Because women in general are lower paid than men, women migrants are more likely than men to accept bad working conditions and poorly paid work. They often get jobs in catering and domestic service, where there is little government regulation and no trade unions. The 'maid trade' is a major part of women's migration: in 2002, up to 1.5 million women were working outside their own countries as foreign maids.

Like other migrants, women who work often send money back to support family left behind. Some women set up businesses that generate income at home and overseas. Moroccan women in Italy are busy building trading links with their home country. Women make a major contribution to the economies of their countries of origin.

WOMEN REFUGEES

Around 50% of the world's refugees are women and girls. The majority have to flee their homes because of war. Others are political activists who oppose repressive governments. Some are in danger because of a relative's political position. Sometimes, women are persecuted for other reasons: because they refuse an arranged marriage, or leave a violent husband, or wear the wrong clothes. In many societies, laws and cultural practices deny women basic human rights.

Women suffer the same forms of persecution as men, but they also suffer particular forms of abuse, such as rape. At the same time, they may lack the money to arrange travel to a safe country. Many women are tricked and exploited by unscrupulous traffickers and people smugglers.

Women and children are more likely than men to end up in large refugee camps on the borders of war-torn countries, where they are very vulnerable.

Women flee their homes for many reasons such as the threat of war, political oppression and persecution.

31

From maid to model

Waris Dirie grew up with a tribe of herdsmen in the Somali desert. She fled when her father announced that he had arranged her marriage to a much older man.

She reached her sister in the capital city, and then got a job as a maid to the Somali ambassador in London. She went to the UK and for four years cooked and cleaned from dawn until bedtime.

When the Ambassador returned to Somalia she hid, and stayed in London. While working at a fast food restaurant she was hired as a model – the start of an international career. She now campaigns on women's issues.

TRAFFICKING OF WOMEN

Up to two million women and children are victims of traffickers each year. Trafficking networks spread across the world: from Nigeria to Italy, the Philippines to South Korea, Kosovo to Belgium, and from Laos to Thailand and Australia.

The women are controlled through debt, drugs, intimidation and imprisonment. If they escape, the authorities sometimes treat them as illegal immigrants, and deport them back to where they came from.

CHILDREN & IMMIGRATION

Children move to other countries for a number of different reasons. Often, it's because their mother or father is going to work abroad. Some are sent on their own, to stay with relatives and go to school. Some children are escaping violence and persecution with their family. Some have to flee on their own. And some are taken by traffickers and forced to work far from home, in terrible conditions.

CHILDREN AS IMMIGRANTS

Many immigrant children arrive in a country legally, to live with an adult who cares for them. Families often move together, though sometimes one adult goes ahead, and the rest follow later. Many governments run 'family reunion' schemes so that relatives can join a settled immigrant.

Some children have to flee on their own and travel to a faraway country where they know no-one.

32

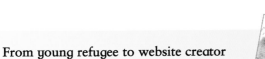

From young refugee to website creator
Sieng Van Tran fled with his family from Vietnam in a small fishing boat in 1979, when he was three years old. They spent two years in a refugee camp in Singapore, before reaching London where they were given refugee status.

Tran went to school. It was hard, but once he learnt English things got better. He went to university and studied artificial intelligence. He came up with an idea for a website that would give people the chance to learn at their own pace, in their own place and in their own time. He spent months developing the project, which he called iLearn.To, in his bedroom.

Tran persuaded a team of financial backers to invest 4.5 million US dollars in the website. He is now on his way to becoming a multi-millionaire. He still spends time helping Vietnamese people in the UK.

CHILDREN AS REFUGEES

Around half the world's refugees are children. Some are with their parents, some are not. Of those who escape on their own, not all are successful in their claim for asylum. In Canada, about half the children who request asylum are given refugee status, but in Europe only five per cent are recognised as refugees. Of those who are turned down, some are allowed to stay on humanitarian grounds.

Some governments and humanitarian agencies help families who get split up to be reunited. The right to family life is considered important in many countries.

CHILDREN AND TRAFFICKING

Trafficking happens when children are handed over to adults who take them to another country and force them to work, or sell them on. They end up in mines, sweatshops and factories. They are made to work as beggars, as servants, on farms and on building sites. They are trafficked for prostitution and pornography. They are forced to be child soldiers and to clear landmines.

These children work for little or no money – they are slaves. Their health suffers and they are abused. The traffickers can make high profits and are rarely caught. Parents often think they have handed their children over to someone who is looking after them. They may never hear from the child again.

WHY DO CHILDREN FLEE?

Children become refugees to escape danger. Their parents may be targeted for speaking out against an unjust government. Their family may belong to an ethnic group or religion that is being persecuted. They may live in a war-torn country. Sometimes, children are themselves under threat. They may be kidnapped and forced into child labour. They may see their families killed. Because of such dangers, parents often try and send their children to safety. Before the Second World War, Jewish parents in Germany and Austria saved their children by putting them on trains and boats to England.

The rights of children

The 1989 International Convention on the Rights of the Child spells out children's rights. Nation states have a responsibility to look after children. It is now recognised that children may be refugees in their own right. Children don't often know this.

Countries are meant to provide protection and help to children, whether they are with their parents or alone. But governments vary in how they cope with child refugees. Some have tough control measures. They X-ray children to check their age, and may deport them. Sometimes they put them in detention centres.

33

Afghan children fled the danger and violence in Afghanistan and many are now immigrants in Pakistan.

Environment & Immigration

Each year, hundreds of thousands of people are affected by natural and man-made disasters, such as floods, droughts, earthquakes and forest fires. In coming years, global warming and climate change will lead to more people fleeing environmental problems.

Though they lose their homes, most people hit by environmental disaster stay in their own country. Others leave to rebuild their lives elsewhere. At the moment, they aren't considered refugees, but people argue that they should be as they are just as in need of help. UNHCR, the main international refugee aid agency, says it does not have the funds to take on millions more people. Campaigners say the wealthy countries should do more to help, because it is the use of fossil fuels in the developed world that is causing global warming.

SINKING ISLAND

Tuvalu is a tiny nation in the Pacific, made up of nine coral atolls. Around 6,000 people – nearly half the population – are crammed onto one 30-hectare atoll which is only three metres above the waves.

34

With global warming causing sea levels to rise, the islanders are slowly leaving. High waves already flood the capital from time to time. The sea also seeps up through holes in the island. New Zealand will take some of the environmental refugees. In the long run, the Tuvalu government says the only solution is to move the whole population overseas.

FLEEING FAMINE AND REPRESSION

Up to 300,000 North Koreans have escaped to China and Mongolia, where they live in secret, hiding from the authorities. They are fleeing famine and repression in their country. Bad management and natural disasters have caused over six years of food shortages and devastating malnutrition in North Korea. As many as three million people have died.

When there is no rain for a long period of time, crops fail and the population may starve without help from international aid agencies.

LETHAL ENVIRONMENTS

After the break-up of the Soviet Union, the new nations were left to face the problems caused by its nuclear weapons programme. Some of the nuclear testing sites and atomic waste disposal sites were emitting radioactive materials. Dozens of towns, and several major cities, were extremely badly affected by industrial pollution.

At least 700,000 people have moved away from dangerous areas. This includes the Chernobyl district, the site of the world's worst nuclear accident.

DESERTIFICATION: CAUSE OF MASS MOVEMENTS

Desertification describes what is happening in many dry regions of the world where people farm and live off the land. The ground is slowly becoming like desert: little or nothing will grow.

Some agencies say that millions of people from Sub-Saharan Africa could leave desertified areas in the next 20 years. Many have already moved because they can no longer grow enough food. Desertification doesn't just happen in Africa.

There are lots of reasons why desertification happens. Poverty means people can't care for the land properly. Lack of irrigation and drought have an impact. Overgrazing and cutting down too many trees are a problem in many places. Population growth adds to the pressure. Unless desertification is addressed, more people will migrate to survive.

VOLCANIC ERUPTION

In the early morning hours of December 26, 1997, the volcano on the Caribbean island of Montserrat erupted. Rock and ash fell on the surrounding villages. A huge cloud of ash blacked out the sun.

Fortunately, a few months earlier the capital city had been hit by an eruption, so people had already left the south of the island. Around 11,000 people lived on Montserrat, and in 1998 nearly half of them left because their homes had been destroyed and they feared more eruptions. Many went to the UK, because of historical links between the two countries.

35

In 1998, Montserrat was devastated by a volcanic eruption. Fortunately, many of the 11,000 people who left have now been able to return.

WHAT GOVERNMENTS DO

As the movement of people around the world has increased, governments have become aware of the need to do more to manage the numbers entering their borders. Some countries are working to limit the number of people crossing their borders. Humanitarian organisations say that wealthy countries should instead be helping the countries of emigration through fair trade and investment.

Governments usually monitor their country's borders.

? Why do governments want to take control?

To help the economy – Mass movements of people place a strain on the economy. Well-managed immigration can be of benefit to a country's economy.

For security – There are concerns about terrorist attacks and international crime.

To secure votes – Immigration is now a hot political issue. Voters in many countries are worried about being 'swamped' by immigrants. In the USA, there is a debate over whether to legalise all illegal immigrants. Some feel that the purpose of this would be to win votes from the Mexican community in the US.

To stop extremist groups – If governments do nothing, anti-immigrant and racist movements may gain popularity.

To meet international obligations – Governments that have signed the Convention on Refugees are required to offer a safe haven to genuine refugees and to respect the rights of immigrants and children.

STOPPING ILLEGAL IMMIGRATION

Many countries are trying to limit the number of people entering their borders. Measures include:

• Fining airlines and airports if they carry people with false documents and strengthening border controls

• Carrying out police raids to find illegal immigrants

• Detaining and deporting illegal immigrants

• Introducing ID cards

• Cutting back state support for asylum seekers

• Cracking down on employers who use illegal labourers

• Imposing harsh prison sentences on people smugglers and traffickers

• Closing refugee camps and closing borders

Sniffer dogs and scanners are used to find people hidden in vehicles crossing borders.

VOICES OF CRITICISM

UN agencies, the International Office for Migration, humanitarian organisations and some economists are critical of the clamp-down on immigration. They say there is a demand for workers, but restrictions are being stepped up because immigration and asylum are politically unpopular. They say that countries need immigrants, and prosper because of them.

When legal forms of migration are limited, people resort to illegal entry, and by making it hard to request asylum, genuine refugees suffer. This may lead to refugees relying on smugglers as their only way to escape. These organisations say that the right to request asylum must be upheld. They call for fair trade and investment in countries of emigration, and for aid to help people overcome poverty.

ENCOURAGING LEGAL MIGRATION

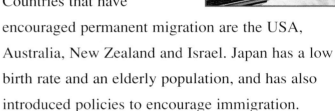

Sometimes governments encourage immigration. In the 1950s, London Transport actively recruited staff in the West Indies to work on buses and underground trains. Countries that have encouraged permanent migration are the USA, Australia, New Zealand and Israel. Japan has a low birth rate and an elderly population, and has also introduced policies to encourage immigration.

Since 2000, the British government has allowed in limited numbers of skilled migrants. It has also allowed in several thousand lower-skilled workers who are needed to work where there is a labour shortage, such as in food processing.

WORKING INTERNATIONALLY

To manage migration, governments have to work together. Members of the European Union, for example, are creating immigration policies, so they have more control over who enters the region. Many governments provide aid directly to countries that migrants are leaving, and some offer more help when there is a major disaster. Most support the UN and international aid agencies that work in areas of conflict and poverty, or that support refugees.

The International Organisation for Migration works on migration issues, and with refugees, all over the world.

37

Migrants waiting outside the Sangatte refugee camp in northern France.

SANGATTE: A CAMP THAT WAS CLOSED

The Sangatte refugee camp in northern France became notorious as a holding centre for migrants trying to the reach the UK. Before the camp opened, the refugees were sleeping rough in parks and on beaches. Inside the camp, up to 1,500 people could be given basic accommodation and food.

There were a number of problems. French shopkeepers didn't like the refugees hanging around in the town. Each night, many of the camp's inhabitants would make an all out effort to enter the Channel Tunnel and reach the UK. Freight train operators said they were losing 15 million pounds every three months through trains being delayed by people in the tunnel.

Eurotunnel, the operator of the rail link, asked the French courts to shut down the centre, and a newspaper in the UK ran a campaign saying that the camp encouraged illegal immigration. Sangatte was closed in 2002, after the French and British governments agreed that half the camp's residents would be admitted to the UK. The others were encouraged to go home voluntarily, or deported.

But new waves of migrants still arrive. Shutting the camp has not stemmed the flow of people.

Stopping the movement of people

Botswana is putting up a 528-kilometre electric fence on part of its border with Zimbabwe, to stop people crossing the border. Uzbekistan has closed an important bridge crossing into Afghanistan.

As a response to September 11, tens of thousands of men from Arab countries living in the USA had to report to immigration authorities to have their papers checked.

They formed long queues at immigration centres, waiting to be finger-printed and photographed. Anyone with out-of-date papers or no documents was detained.

The Australian navy has intercepted boats carrying refugees to prevent them landing on its shores. The government puts the asylum seekers into remote camps, where the conditions are very harsh.

WHAT IMMIGRANTS DO

Most migrants end up doing dirty, difficult and dangerous jobs. In some countries, immigrants earn less than local people even when they are doing the same jobs. People who are in the country illegally are much more likely to be exploited than legal migrants. However, most end up earning more than they would have done at home.

LOW-PAID AND INSECURE

Migrants tend to do the work that local people don't want to take on. These are the sectors they often work in:

Construction – Many migrants work on building sites. This is an industry that goes through periods of boom and decline. It needs people it can take on and lay off easily. The work is often hard, dangerous, and short term.

Agriculture – Farms need seasonal workers to pick the harvest. Much of the work has to be done by hand. There is also work in packaging factories.

Work done by immigrants can be very dangerous.

Personal services – This covers a range of work, from nursing and childcare to cleaning and gardening.

Factory work – Legal migrants may get secure jobs in well-regulated factories where there are decent working conditions. Others end up in small sweatshops where workers have to put in long hours in terrible conditions.

Once, these jobs would have been done by women and children. But in developed countries, women have become better educated and they want better jobs. Birth rates are declining, and more people go to university: there aren't as many young people to do the low-paid work. So, jobs that were traditionally done by local people are filled by immigrant workers. In New York in the 1980s, for example, the taxis were driven by people born in the USA. Now, more than 90% of New York taxi drivers are foreign born.

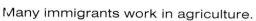
Many immigrants work in agriculture.

Immigrants in Singapore

Singapore is an example of a country dependent on foreign-born workers. There has been a labour shortage there since the 1960s. In the 1990s, there were more than 300,000 legal migrants in the country. They included:

• 180,000 Malaysians, working mostly in factories and the shipping industry

• 50,000 Thais, working on roads and building sites (nearly half of these didn't have the right documents)

• 40,000 women from the Philippines, mostly in domestic work

• 20,000 Bangladeshis and other South Asian nationals, working in construction

• 10,000 professionals and business men

Though they are a vital part of the economy, the lower-paid workers face many problems. Their health suffers through long hours, bad conditions and poor diet. Many are struggling to pay off the cost of travelling to Singapore and getting papers. Illegal immigrants in particular earn scarcely enough to survive.

CROP-PICKING IN THE UK

Over 100,000 people work for gangmasters on farms and in the food packing industry in the UK. The government has acknowledged that without migrant labour the industry would collapse. The workers come from China, Bulgaria, Russia, Lithuania, Pakistan, Portugal, Yemen and other countries. Most have entered the UK illegally. Asylum seekers in the UK are not allowed to work, but some of them also pick crops. They and the illegal immigrants work 12-hour shifts for less than the minimum wage. Some pay rent to gangmasters to live in overcrowded accommodation.

In February 2004, 19 Chinese migrant workers drowned whilst picking cockles in Morecambe Bay, England. They were caught by the dangerous fast-rising tide. They were working for gangmasters who profit from the immigrants, and make them work in conditions which can be extremely dangerous.

40

THE BRAIN DRAIN

Highly educated and professional people become international migrants. More are migrating now than ten years ago. They head for the cities and centres of business where they can earn well and develop their careers. Around 70,000 African professionals and university graduates go to Europe and North America each year. European scientists, engineers and computer experts leave to live in the USA.

The brain drain is not all bad news. It can encourage trade. Some professionals return to their home country years later, more qualified and more experienced.

Thousands of professional people migrate each year in search of better salaries, careers and working conditions.

Outworkers in Australia

Tran and Lam are Vietnamese refugees living in Australia. They work at a friend's house, making clothes for a number of different brand names. They work on average 12 to 14 hours a day. Their four children help them. The younger ones fold the clothes and cut threads, the older ones work at sewing machines. The children work about three hours a night, and more at the weekend.

The contractors are always pushing for the work to be done more quickly. The pay is in cash. By working long hours, the family has just enough to live on.

GOOD FOR THE ECONOMY?

Migrants send money home, and they spend money in the country they have moved to. In 2001, there were 23 million Mexicans and people of Mexican origin living in the USA, both legally and without documents. This is how they helped the economies of the two countries:

• They sent about nine billion US dollars to Mexico.

• This was only about 15 per cent of their income – the rest they spent locally.

• This means that the Mexican community contributes close to 82 billion dollars a year to the US economy.

Most organisations employ foreign-born workers.

41

ACTIVELY SEEKING PROFESSIONALS

The UK's National Health Service (NHS) is one of the largest employers in Europe. There is a shortage of British doctors, nurses and midwives, and the service actively recruits health workers from overseas.

The arrival of foreign doctors and nurses is good for the NHS, but it has a damaging impact on the level of care in the health workers' home countries. The British government has said the NHS must not recruit from almost all of the developing countries.

Leaving Zimbabwe

Abel is a newly-qualified doctor working in a hospital in Harare, the capital of Zimbabwe. He is planning to move to Australia to find work. He says he doesn't have the drugs and equipment he needs to save lives. He wants to work in modern conditions, and to earn enough to support his family.

More than 80 per cent of doctors, nurses and therapists who graduated from the University of Zimbabwe since 1980 have gone to work abroad.

GOING HOME

Some people return to their original country when conditions improve.

Twenty years ago, most international migration was between particular countries, and it was long-term. People settled permanently in the country they moved to. Young men who left Pakistan in the 1950s to work in the mill towns of Northern England made it their home. Now the picture is more complicated. People travel to work abroad for short periods. Some people move from one country to another – some end up back where they started. Others live many decades abroad, and go back to their original country when they retire. Sometimes, one generation settles permanently overseas, but their grandchildren end up moving back to the country their grandparents came from.

Going back to Kosovo

Zoran is one of nearly 200,000 ethnic Serbs and Romas who fled Kosovo in 1999. In 2003, he was among the first to go back to his village. Many people stay away because they fear the ethnic Albanian majority.

When he returned, the door and windows to his house were gone. Some other Serbs joined him soon after, and community relations in the village are good. However, the Serbs feel uneasy travelling to the nearby town, and they don't make use of the health centre there. UNHCR and other agencies have distributed food, delivered beds, firewood and stoves, and have helped with repairs.

RETURNING REFUGEES

Many refugees hope to go home when their country is safe. The journey can be expensive, and they may find they have lost their house and possessions, and have to start all over again. Sometimes, the situation they return to is still insecure.

In 2002 and 2003, 2.5 million refugees returned to Afghanistan from Pakistan and Iran. Most were helped by the UNHCR and aid organisations. In Africa, refugees are being helped to return to countries ravaged by war. Often, aid agencies work closely with governments to make travel arrangements and to set up work and housing programmes.

The UNHCR helps refugees to return to their country of origin.

NEW COUNTRY, NEW HOME

While many people go back to their country of origin, others never return. They settle, work and raise families, and some apply to be citizens of the country they have moved to. This means that they can vote in elections, and they have the same rights and responsibilities as other citizens. They are issued with a passport by their adopted country. In some countries, such as the USA and Canada, long-term immigrants are encouraged to take this step. In others, it can be much harder to become a citizen.

The impact of immigration

Throughout history, immigrants and their descendants have changed our world.
• John Fitzgerald Kennedy (JFK), the youngest US president ever elected, was descended from Irish great-grandparents.
• Famous and influential refugees include Roberto Goizuetta (the former CEO of Coca Cola), Salvador Dali (artist), Edward Said (Palestinian author and academic), Sigmund Freud (founder of psychoanalysis), Frederic Chopin (composer) and Victor Hugo (author of 'Les Miserables' and 'The Hunchback of Notre Dame'). (See page 17).

Many migrants desperately want to be able to return to their own country and live there without fear of persecution, war or starvation.

43

FORCED TO RETURN

Across the world, illegal immigrants and asylum seekers are deported from countries they have entered. For asylum seekers, this may happen when their request for asylum is officially turned down, or they may be turned away at a border because they arrive with false documents or no papers at all.

The deportees may be returned to their country of origin. This is called repatriation. This can have serious consequences if the deportee faces persecution in the country they go back to.

For example, thousands of Burmese people working illegally in Thailand face punishment and forced labour if they are sent back to Burma.

Asylum seekers are increasingly being sent away from countries where governments are tightening controls. In 2002, Germany and other western European countries deported Chechen asylum seekers on the grounds that conditions there had improved. Human rights groups said that the Chechens faced a daily threat of being detained and tortured.

CHRONOLOGY

700,000 BC – Early man started moving into Europe from Africa.

700,000-80,000 BC – People continued to migrate across Europe.

35,000-10,000 BC – A new species, *Homo sapiens* (humans), entered Europe from the Near East. They started off in southern and central Europe and moved northwards as the glaciers melted.

400 BC-500 AD – The Roman Empire spread over large parts of Europe. Christians fled from the Roman-occupied countries, where they were persecuted, and became refugees.

800-1100 – Vikings (Nordic people) swarmed across Europe from Scandinavia. Some of them even got as far as North America.

1492 – Christopher Columbus reached the Americas. This began European colonisation of America and paved the way for mass immigration.

late 1400s-1865 – Around 15 million Africans were transported to America against their will where they were forced to work as slaves. In total, up to 28 million people were taken from Africa to work as slaves in various parts of the world.

Early 1600s – Many immigrants crossed from Europe to North America. The voyage took between 6 and 12 weeks, during which many people died of disease.

1620 – The Mayflower crossed the Atlantic from Plymouth, England, to Cape Cod in North America. The ship carried 102 passengers, known as the Pilgrims.

Late 1600s-1800s – Hundreds of thousands of Huguenots (Protestants) fled from France to Protestant parts of America and Europe, including Britain, Switzerland, Germany, Denmark and the Dutch Republic. They did this following the massacre of Huguenot leaders in 1572.

1788-1868 – Around 162,000 convicts (prisoners) were sent to Australia from England and Ireland.

1807 – The slave trade was banned in Britain.

1820-1924 – Between 35 and 40 million Europeans emigrated to America. They went there as demand for labourers increased after the abolition of the slave trade. They also wanted a better standard of living.

1846-1850 – The Irish Potato Famine took as many as one million lives. It spurred the emigration of up to two million people to North America, England, Wales and Scotland.

1861-1865 – The American Civil War; its end marked the abolition of slavery in the USA.

1917-1925 – Around 1.5 million people left Russia to escape communist repression, starvation and war.

1922-1975 – Decolonisation of the English, French, Dutch, Portuguese, German, Italian and Flemish colonies resulted in migration of people back to their 'motherland'.

1930-1942 – The number of Jews that left German-occupied countries as a result of Hitler's regime was over 300,000.

1947 – The partition of India (the dividing of the Indian subcontinent into India and Pakistan, following the departure of the British government) caused large-scale emigration. Hindus, Christians, Muslims and Sikhs left the subcontinent to settle in the UK.

1948 – Israel was founded and war broke out between the Israelis and the Arabs. Jews moved to Israel from all over Europe. By 1966, there were 2.6 million Jews in Israel compared to only 300,000 Palestinians.

1948 – The General Assembly of the United Nations adopted and proclaimed the Universal Declaration of Human Rights. Amongst many other things, this declaration gave everyone the right to leave their country and to seek asylum in other countries to escape persecution.

1951 – The Convention relating to the Status of Refugees created laws to protect refugees. In this year there were one million refugees or displaced people worldwide, according to the UNHCR.

1960 onwards – Many immigrant labourers brought their families to the Western countries in which they had settled. Governments encouraged family reunions.

1980 – Around 8.2 million refugees and displaced people worldwide.

1989 – The fall of the Berlin Wall stimulated migration of around 218,000 Germans from Eastern Europe to Germany. This figure is actually much less than was expected.

1989-1994 – Around 700,000 refugees from the former Yugoslavia fled to Western Europe. The other 4.3 million refugees and displaced people are still living in the states that emerged from the break-up of Yugoslavia.

1991 – The Gulf War. Nearly two million people fled to neighbouring countries from Iraq.

1995 – Around 26 million refugees and displaced people worldwide.

2002 – US refugee approvals for asylum fell by 72 per cent following tightened controls due to the September 11th attacks in New York and Washington DC.

Mid 2002-Mid 2003 – Up to 1.5 million West Africans were forced to leave their homes because of war.

2002 – In total, there were 327,142 applications for asylum in the 25 main industrialised countries between January and September.

2003 – Around 20 million refugees and displaced people worldwide.

2003 – Between January and September, the largest group of asylum seekers were from Russia. The majority of these people were Chechens escaping conflict in their country. The second largest group of asylum seekers were from Iraq.

ORGANISATIONS AND GLOSSARY

Anti-Slavery International
Thomas Clarkson House
The Stableyard
Broomgrove Road
London
SW9 9TL
UK
Tel: +44 (0)20 7501 8920
Fax: +44 (0)20 7738 4110
Email: info@antislavery.org
Website: www.antislavery.org
Anti-Slavery International works at local, national and international levels to eliminate the system of slavery around the world.

Canadian Council for Refugees
6839 Drolet
#302
Montréal
Québec
H2S 2T1
Canada
Tel: +1 (514) 277-7223
Fax: +1 (514) 277-1447
E-mail: ccr@web.net
Website: www.web.net/~ccr/
The Canadian Council for Refugees is a non-profit making organisation committed to the rights and protection of refugees in Canada and around the world, and to the settlement of refugees and immigrants in Canada.

Human Rights Watch
350 Fifth Avenue, 34th floor
New York
NY 10118-3299
USA
Tel: +1 (212) 290 4700
Fax: +1 (212) 736 1300
Email: hrwnyc@hrw.org
Website: www.hrw.org
Human Rights Watch protects the human rights of people worldwide. They investigate and expose human rights violations and hold abusers accountable. They challenge governments and those who hold power to end abusive practices and respect international human rights law.

International Organisation for
Migration (IOM)
17, Route des Morillons
CH-1211
Geneva 19
Switzerland
Tel: +41 22 717 9111
Fax: +41 22 798 6150
Email: hq@iom.int
Website: www.iom.int
IOM is one of the leading international organisations for migration. It works to increase understanding of migration issues, encourage social and economic development through migration, and to uphold the human dignity and well-being of migrants.

National Network for Immigrant and
Refugee Rights
310 Eighth Street
Suite 303
Oakland
CA 94607
USA
Tel: +1 510 465 1984
Fax: +1 510 465 1885
Email: nnirr@nnirr.org
Website: www.nnirr.org
The National Network for Immigrant and Refugee Rights (NNIRR) is a national organisation made up of immigrant, refugee, and other organisations.

Refugee Council
3 Bondway
London SW8 1SJ
UK
Tel: +44 (0)20 7820 3000
Fax: +44 (0)20 7582 9929
Email: info@refugeecouncil.org.uk
Website: www.refugeecouncil.org.uk

Refugee Council of Australia
PO Box 946
Glebe 2037
NSW
Australia
Tel: +61 2 9660-5300
Fax: +61 2 9660-5211
Email: info@refugeecouncil.org.au
Website: www.refugeecouncil.org.au

Sweatshop Watch
310 Eighth Street
Suite 303
Oakland
CA 94607
USA
Tel: +1 510 834 8990
Email: sweatinfo@sweatshopwatch.org
Website: www.sweatshopwatch.org
Sweatshop Watch is a coalition of over 30 organisations, and many individuals, committed to eliminating the exploitation that occurs in sweatshops.

United Nations High Commissioner
for Refugees (UNHCR)
Case Postal 2500
CH-1211
Geneva 2
Switzerland
Tel: +41 22 739 8111
Fax: +41 22 739 7314/15/16
Email: hqpi00@unhcr.ch
Website: www.unhcr.ch
UNHCR is the lead agency for the protection of displaced people and refugees. It upholds the rights of refugees, runs refugee camps, and helps refugees returning home.

Other useful websites:

www.bbc.co.uk

Search BBC news for country profiles and news items on migration and refugees around the world.

www.movinghere.org.uk

Interactive website which documents 200 years of Caribbean, Irish, Jewish and South Asian migration to the UK.

www.endchildexploitation.org.uk

A campaign run by UNICEF UK to end child exploitation worldwide.

ORGANISATIONS AND GLOSSARY

Aid
Money or support given to countries in need by governments and charities.

Asylum
A shelter from danger or hardship.

Asylum seeker
Someone seeking asylum or refugee status in another country because they fear persecution at home.

Border
The boundary of a country.

Citizen
A person who has a legal right to live in a country, vote for its government and is protected by its laws.

Civilian
Someone who is not part of the army, navy or airforce.

Colony
A country that is under the rule of another country.

Conscription
Compulsory enrolment in the armed forces.

Developed countries
Countries that are technologically advanced, highly urbanised (built-up) and wealthy.

Developing countries
Countries in the process of becoming industrialised.

Economic migrant
Someone moving to a country, intending to work there.

Emigration
When people leave a country.

Ethnic cleansing
Eradicating everyone from an ethnic group, through persecution and murder.

Genocide
The killing of everyone who belongs to a particular ethnic or national group.

Global warming
An increase in the average temperature of the Earth's surface, which occurs following an increase in greenhouse gases (mainly carbon dioxide).

Illegal immigrant
Someone in another country, who does not have the necessary official papers.

Immigrant
Someone who has settled in a country in order to live and work there, usually for a few years or longer.

Immigration
The process of people arriving at, and passing through, border controls in a foreign country, with the intention of staying there for a while.

International migration
The movement of people across a border, in order to stay there a while.

Migration
The movement of people from one area or country to another in search of work or a different lifestyle.

Nation
A people or land area under the rule of one government.

Persecution
Hunting people down, harassing and sometimes killing them, because of their beliefs or because they belong to a particular group.

Racism
Discriminating against people on the basis of their skin colour or ethnic origin.

Refugee
Someone who has fled their country and has been granted asylum in another country, in accordance with international law.

Smuggler
Someone who gets people across borders illegally.

Sweatshop
A small workshop where people work long hours, in bad conditions, for little pay. They are often linked to the clothing industry.

Trafficking
The moving of people for profit, often against their will.

Transnational companies
Companies that have offices or factories in several countries.

Undocumented worker
Someone who has travelled abroad to work, but does not have the official papers needed to stay in a country.